W9-CMJ-115

Wild Animal Kingdom

KILLER WHALES

GAIL TERP

BLACK
RABBIT
BOOKS

Bolt is published by Black Rabbit Books
P.O. Box 3263, Mankato, Minnesota, 56002.
www.blackrabbitbooks.com
Copyright © 2017 Black Rabbit Books

Design and Production by Michael Sellner
Photo Research by Rhonda Milbrett

Library of Congress Control Number: 2015954872

HC ISBN: 978-1-68072-052-5   PB ISBN: 978-1-68072-309-0

Printed in the United States at CG Book Printers,
North Mankato, Minnesota, 56003. PO #1798 4/16

Image Credits
Biosphoto: Christopher Swann, 17 (top); Corbis: Brandon Hauser/ SuperStock, Cover; Pablo Cersosimo/robertharding, 16; Theo Allofs, 4–5; Dreamstime: Krystof, 28–29; Flickr: Carla Meo, 13 (bottom); istock: hanhanpeggy, 32; Musat, Back Cover, 1, 6, 22–23 (center); photoworks1, 24; sethakan, 9 (bottom); sanfrancisco.cbslocal.com: Sheila Semans, 27; Shutterstock: Airin.dizain, 18–19 (silhouettes); Mike Liu, 15; Monika Wieland, 22 (top), 23 (bottom); Nerthuz, 6–7; pr2is, 9 (top); Rich Carey, 25; Stephen Lew, 13 (top); TOSP, 3, 14; Triduza Studio, 10–11, 31; Superstock: Biosphoto, 17 (bottom); Gerard Lacz/age fotostock, 21
Every effort has been made to contact copyright holders for material reproduced in this book. Any omissions will be rectified in subsequent printings if notice is given to the publisher.

Contents

CHAPTER 1

A Day in the Life

A **pod** of killer whales hunts for its next meal. The whales call quietly to each other. Their large black and white bodies glide through the water. They come to an icy beach.

One whale lifts partway from the water. It sees a group of seals on the beach. The whales make a huge wave. The waves wash seals into the water. Lunch!

9,500
8,000   11,000
6,500   12,500
4,500   14,000
3,000   15,500
1,500 ——————— 17,000
pounds **WEIGHT** pounds

**4,200 TO 12,333
POUNDS**
(1,905 TO 5,594
KILOGRAMS)

Food and Fun

The whales share their catch of seals. Then it's time to play. They call loudly to each other. They leap and splash in the waves.

How Big Is a Killer Whale?

LENGTH
19 TO 27 FEET
(6 to 8 meters)

Orcas

Killer whales are not actually whales. They are part of the dolphin family. Many people prefer to call these animals orcas. Like dolphins, killer whales are playful. When two pods meet, the animals might play together.

• •

A killer whale breathes through a **blowhole**. This hole opens when the whale comes up for air.

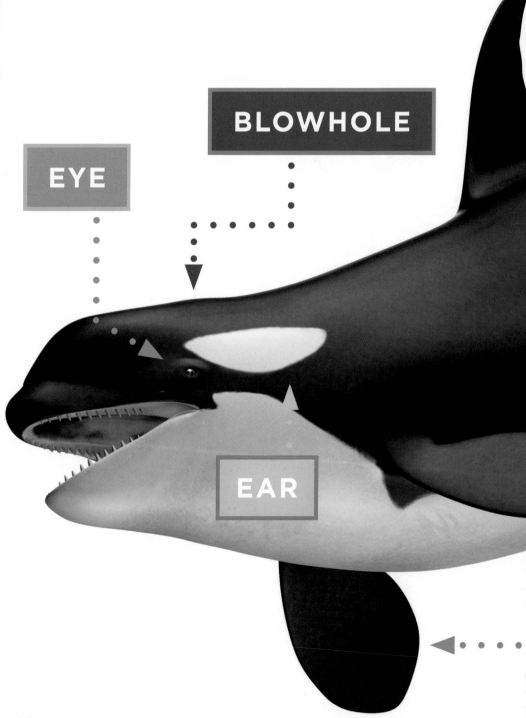

BLOWHOLE

EYE

EAR

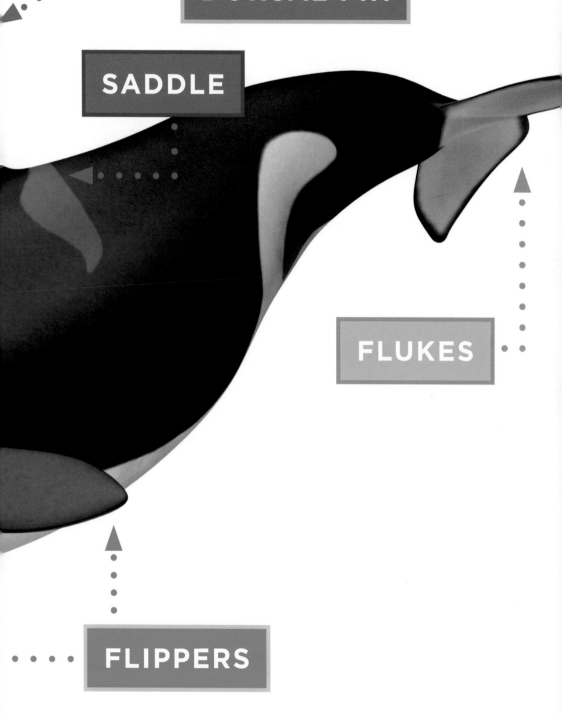

DORSAL FIN

SADDLE

FLUKES

FLIPPERS

CHAPTER 2

Food to Eat
and a Place to Live

Killer whales eat fish and sea birds. They also eat seals and whales. They swallow most **prey** whole.

A killer whale uses sound to find prey. First, it sends out clicks. Then it listens. The clicks bounce off nearby prey. The bounced clicks help the whale know where food is.

Smart Thinking

Killer whales don't use clicks to hunt other mammals. When they hear noises from the other animals, they close in.

By the Numbers

12.4 POUNDS (5.6 KG)
WEIGHT OF BRAIN

30 MILES (48 KM) PER HOUR
TOP SWIM SPEED

3 TO 4 INCHES (8 TO 10 CM)
LENGTH OF EACH TOOTH

40 TO 56 TEETH

50 to 80 YEARS LIFE SPAN

LONGEST KILLER WHALE 32.3 FEET (9.8 M)

MORE THAN
20,000
POUNDS
(9,072 KG)

HEAVIEST
KILLER WHALE

Living and Working Together

Killer whales live in all the world's oceans. Some are found in **bays** and the **mouths** of rivers too. They prefer cold water. Their thick **blubber** keeps them warm.

Killer whales work together when they hunt. They come at prey from all sides. They close in. Then all at once, the whales strike. They share their catches.

Hunting Prey

Step 1

work together

Step 2

surround prey

Step 3

strike all at once

WHERE KILLER WHALES LIVE

Killer Whale Range Map

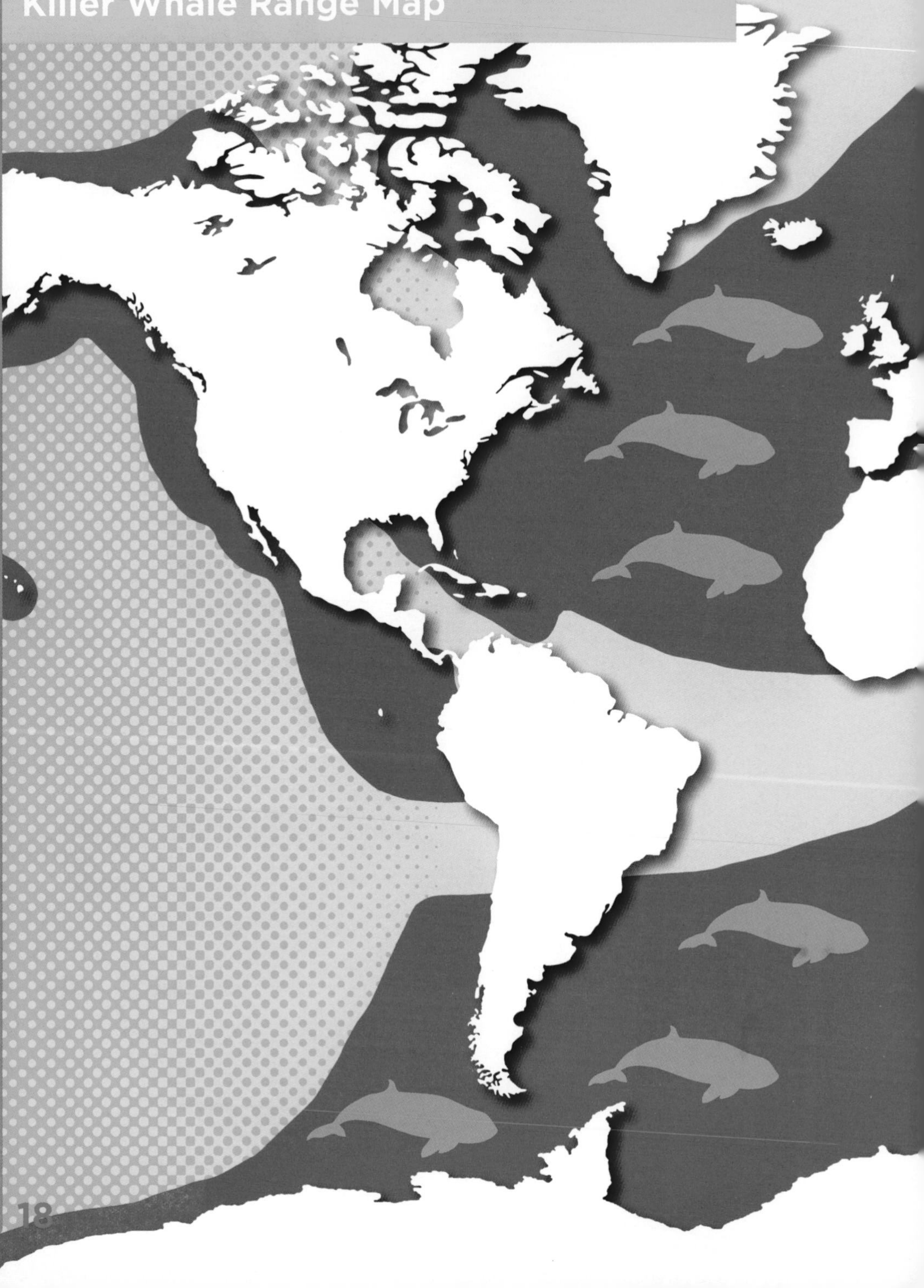

CHAPTER 3

Family Life

Killer whales live in pods. Some pods have only a few whales. Other pods have up to 50 whales. Each pod is led by a female. Whales often stay in their pods for life.

Killer whales give birth at all times of the year. A newborn calf is about 8 feet (2 m) long. It weighs about 300 pounds (136 kg). All the whales help care for the calves. They help feed them. They teach them to hunt too.

spyhop

lifting its head
out of the water

22

leaping out of the water and splashing down breach

smacking the fin on the water

fin slap

CHAPTER 4

Predators
and Other Threats

Killer whales have no **predators**. Humans are their main threat. People **pollute** the water. They cause noise too. This noise makes it hard for whales to hear prey.

Pollution Problems

Pollution makes the whales sick. It also kills other ocean animals. Fewer ocean animals means less food for whales to eat. Pollution also makes females have fewer calves.

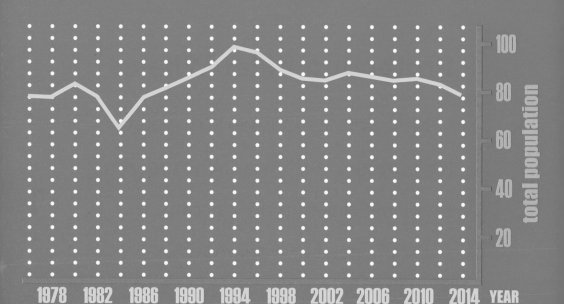

total population

KILLER WHALE POPULATION
in Puget Sound near Washington state

Protecting Killer Whales

Killer whales are smart. They know how to survive all over the world. But they can't clean up their oceans.

People need to work to make the oceans clean. Then these awesome animals can thrive in the world's oceans.

29

bay (BAY)—a small body of water set off from the main body of water

blowhole (BLOW-hole)—a breathing hole in the top of a whale's head

blubber (BLUB-uhr)—the fat on whales and other large sea mammals

mouth (MOWTH)—the place where a river enters the ocean

pod (POD)—a group of whales or dolphins

pollute (PUH-loot)—to spoil with waste made by humans

predator (PRED-uh-tuhr)—an animal that eats other animals

prey (PRAY)—an animal hunted or killed for food

Books

Allyn, Daisy. *Killer Whales Are Not Whales!* Confusing Creature Names. New York: Gareth Stevens Publishing, 2015.

Riggs, Kate. *Killer Whales*. Amazing Animals. Mankato, MN: Creative Education, 2012.

Simon, Charnan, and Ariel Kazunas. *Killer Whales*. Nature's Children. New York: Children's Press, 2013.

Websites

Killer Whale
www.kidsplanet.org/factsheets/orca.html

Killer Whales
www.afsc.noaa.gov/nmml/education/cetaceans/ killer.php

Orca
kids.nationalgeographic.com/animals/orca/